Surviving Hurricanes

Elizabeth Raum

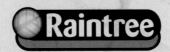

Chicago, Illinois

www.heinemannraintree.com
Visit our website to find out more information about Heinemann-Raintree books.

To order:

☎ Phone 888-454-2279

💻 Visit www.heinemannraintree.com to browse our catalog and order online.

Edited by Louise Galpine and Laura Knowles
Designed by Victoria Allen
Original illustrations © Capstone Global Library Limited 2011
Illustrated by HLSTUDIOS
Picture research by Ruth Blair

Originated by Capstone Global Library Limited
Printed and bound in China by CTPS

15 14 13 12 11
10 9 8 7 6 5 4 3 2 1

Library of Congress Cataloging-in-Publication Data
Raum, Elizabeth.
  Surviving hurricanes / Elizabeth Raum.
    p. cm.—(Children's true stories : natural disasters)
  Includes bibliographical references and index.
  ISBN 978-1-4109-4093-3—ISBN 978-1-4109-4100-8
(pbk.) 1. Hurricanes—Juvenile literature. 2. Emergency management—Juvenile literature. I. Title.
  QC944.2.R38 2012
  363.34'922—dc22   2010036214

Acknowledgments
We would like to thank the following for permission to reproduce photographs: © Antony Haywood p. **15**; Alamy p. **18** (© Danita Delimont); © Corbis p. **11**; Corbis pp. **4** (© Daniel LeClair/Reuters), **13** (© Bettmann), **14** (© Bettmann), **17** (© Smiley N. Pool/Dallas Morning News), **19** (© Lee Celano/Reuters), **20** (© Jerry McCrea/Star Ledger), **21** (© Michael Macor/San Francisco Chronicle), **23** (© Abir Abdullah/epa), **24** (© Abir Abdullah/epa), **25** (© Rafiqur Rahman/Reuters); Library of Congress pp. **7**, **8** (M.H. Zahner), **9** (C.H. Graves), **10**; © NOAA p. **27**; Shutterstock p. **26** (© Jayne Chapman).

Cover photograph of residents of Cangnan county braving strong winds and heavy rain, brought by Typhoon Haitang, in Cangnan county in east China's Zhejiang province, reproduced with permission of Corbis/© China Newsphoto/Reuters.

Lamia's story on page 22 is from ActionAid, www.actionaid. org.uk/doc_lib/lamia_climate_heroine.pdf.

The author would like to thank Antony Haywood and Christopher Nungesser for so generously sharing their stories.

We would like to thank Daniel Block for his invaluable help in the preparation of this book.

Contents

DAILY LIFE

Read here to learn about what life was like for the children in these stories, and the impact the disaster had at home and school.

NUMBER CRUNCHING

Find out here the details about natural disasters and the damage they cause.

Survivors' lives

Read these boxes to find out what happened to the children in this book when they grew up.

HELPING HAND

Find out how people and organizations have helped to save lives.

On the scene

Read eyewitness accounts of the natural disasters in the survivors' own words.

Some words are printed in bold, **like this**. You can find out what they mean by looking in the glossary on page 30.

Introduction

Hurricanes are the biggest storms on Earth. Some hurricanes are 800 kilometers (500 miles) across.

A hurricane is a strong tropical storm. Tropical storms form over warm ocean waters near the **equator**. As the water **evaporates**, it quickly rises and releases energy. Other air moves in at great speed to take the place of the rising air, creating a strong wind. As the wind circles, it draws more and more **moisture** from the ocean's surface. When the storm crosses cold water or land, it loses power and fades away. However, if the storm remains over warm water, it becomes larger and more powerful. When the winds reach speeds of 120 kilometers (74 miles) per hour, the storm is called a **tropical cyclone**.

Hurricane Emily slammed the Mexican coast in 2005.

Hurricane, typhoon, or cyclone?

The term "tropical cyclone" is used worldwide. People in the United States and Europe call these storms hurricanes. In Asia and Australia, the terms "typhoon" or "cyclone" are used.

Hurricanes are frightening. Children who have lived through hurricanes always remember their fear of the storm—and their relief at surviving it.

NUMBER CRUNCHING

This is the Saffir–Simpson Hurricane Wind Scale. It is based on wind speed, which is measured in kilometers or miles per hour.

Intensity of hurricane	Wind speed	Damage that may occur
Category 1	119–152 km/h (74–95 mph)	Tree branches down; unanchored mobile homes damaged; some coastal flooding
Category 2	154–177 km/h (96–110 mph)	Mobile homes and poorly constructed buildings destroyed; small trees down; damage to piers and small boats
Category 3	178–209 km/h (111–130 mph)	Small buildings destroyed; small trees down; some inland flooding; damage to piers, docks, and boats
Category 4	211–249 km/h (131–155 mph)	Outer walls, doors, and windows severely damaged; roofs and small buildings destroyed; trees down; erosion of beaches; inland flooding
Category 5	Over 249 km/h (Over 155 mph)	Many roofs and some buildings destroyed; severe window and door damage; major flooding with water on lower floors of buildings; many people must be **evacuated**

Galveston, Texas: 1900

Sarah Littlejohn, who was eight years old in 1900, lived in Galveston, Texas. Galveston sits on an island in the Gulf of Mexico, about 3.2 kilometers (2 miles) off the coast of Texas. The summer of 1900 had been one of the hottest on record. Finally, on Saturday, September 8, a cool breeze began to blow.

Sarah spent that Saturday morning playing with her friend, Minnie Borden. In the afternoon, Minnie went home, and Sarah's father returned from work. He had news. He had spoken with the local **meteorologist**, who was **predicting** a hurricane. Like most people in Galveston, Sarah's family would stay at home and wait for the storm to pass. There was no safe place to go.

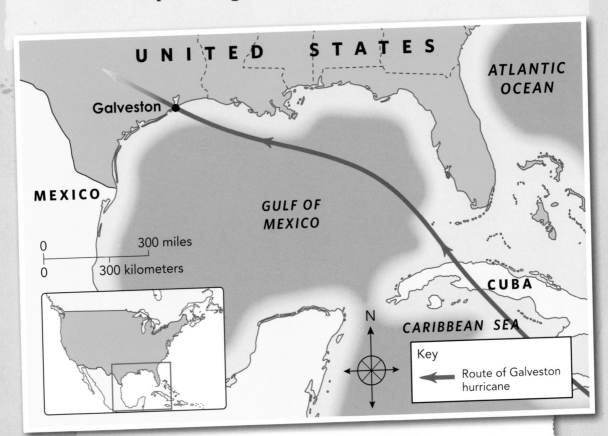

The hurricane that hit Galveston crossed over Cuba on its way west.

DAILY LIFE

In 1900 meteorologists watched the sky and the ocean for clues about the weather. They measured air temperature, wind speeds, and **air pressure**. High temperatures, high wind speeds, and low pressures may indicate that a powerful storm is on the way. Today, meteorologists also depend on **radar** and satellite pictures of storm systems. Weather predicting has improved since 1900.

The huge floods that can accompany hurricanes are strong enough to force houses from their foundations.

A scream in the night

The **tide** was high. Waves crashed against the shore. Soon, water filled the streets of Galveston. Strong winds blew shutters off houses, carried away sheds, and sent tree branches flying. Sarah's father helped neighbors to nail windows and doors shut.

By 6:00 p.m. that evening, water covered the first floor of Sarah's house. When everyone went upstairs, they found that the roof was leaking and the beds were wet. They crowded into the bathroom to stay dry. Sarah heard someone scream. She later wrote, "The sounds we heard that night were just dreadful."

Children had nowhere to go after the Galveston hurricane. This boy is playing around in **debris** left by the disaster.

Destruction all around

When her mother looked out of the window, she saw something large and white float by. It was the house next door. Before the night was over, thousands of homes were destroyed. Sarah's family and their house survived the storm.

On the scene

The **storm surge** destroyed everything between Sarah's house and the beach. She wrote, "The water went down very rapidly, and soon it was daylight Sunday morning. We looked out of the window, and of all the beautiful houses between our house and the beach, not one was left."

In the chaos after the storm, many people did not know where help would come from. Here, supply wagons are delivering much-needed food supplies.

Disaster

The Galveston hurricane is the worst natural disaster in U.S. history. More than 6,000 people drowned or were killed by flying debris. The Category 4 hurricane destroyed 3,636 houses. For the survivors, there was no clean water to drink and very little food. The Red Cross and other relief groups rushed to help.

Rebuilding

When the people of Galveston rebuilt their city, they built a **seawall** to protect against high waves. **Engineers** began to raise the level of the city by 5 meters (17 feet) at the seawall to prevent flooding. It was a huge job, but it helped protect Galveston from future disasters.

In 1904 a man stands on top of a portion of Galveston's new seawall.

On the scene

Clara Barton wrote letters to the U.S. government from Galveston about the flood. On September 18, 1900, she wrote, "There seems to be an unusually large number of children with no one to care for them or who knows them. We will help them as far as possible, gather them in, and the world will give them homes."

Clara Barton was head of the American Red Cross in 1900.

HELPING HAND

New York City children raised $27,907 (over $712,000 in today's dollars) to help the children of Galveston.

Darwin, Australia: 1974

On December 24, 1974, eight-year-old Antony Haywood went to bed dreaming about Christmas presents. He did not know that a hurricane was headed for his hometown of Darwin, Australia. The storm had formed in the Arafura Sea, northeast of Darwin. As **meteorologists** at the **Tropical Cyclone** Warning Center watched, the storm slowed and seemed to be turning away. Then it looped back toward Darwin.

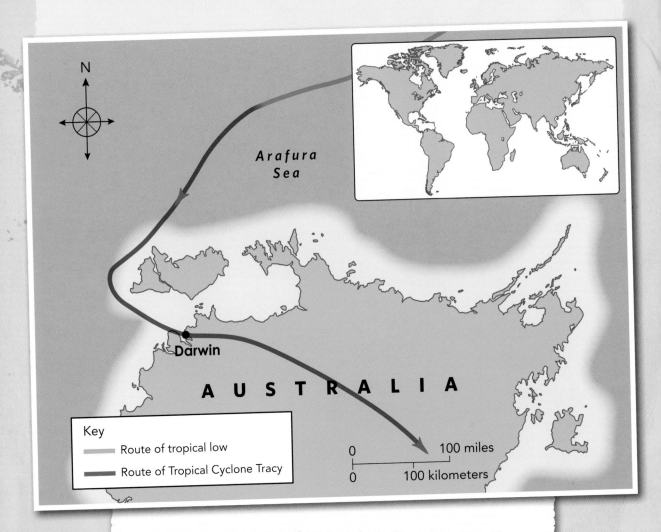

Darwin is on the coast of Australia's Northern Territory. This map shows the path of Cyclone Tracy.

Midnight visitor

Cyclone Tracy, a Category 5 hurricane, struck the city of Darwin at midnight. Antony's mother woke Antony and his younger brother, Steve, just before midnight. She rushed the boys into her bedroom, wrapped them in blankets, and pushed them under her big bed. Then she crawled in beside them. Steve fell asleep—but not Antony. The wind howled, windows shattered, and water dripped onto his face.

Few houses remained standing after the hurricane.

HELPING HAND

Antony's mother chose wisely. The bedroom had three brick walls. Hiding beneath the big bed offered protection against broken glass and flying **debris**. "I was scared," Antony said, "but Mom told us we would be OK, which made me feel much better."

After the hurricane passed, these people walked the streets of Darwin, looking at the damage.

A pile of bricks

When morning arrived, Antony, Steve, and their mother crawled out of the wreckage. They had survived, but the house was just a pile of bricks.

Antony refused to leave home. After all, it was Christmas Day. He searched for the presents that had been underneath the Christmas tree. All he found was a broken action figure for his brother, a toy gun for himself, and a blouse with flowers on it for his mother. It was all they had left.

NUMBER CRUNCHING
This chart shows the damage caused by Cyclone Tracy:

Deaths	Injuries	Ships lost at sea	Buildings destroyed	**Evacuees**
66	790	21	around 10,000	around 35,000

Evacuating

Cyclone Tracy destroyed Darwin. It is one of the worst natural disasters in Australia's history. Most people **evacuated**, or they left Darwin immediately after the storm. Antony and his family moved in with relatives in Perth, Western Australia. People across the country provided temporary homes, supplies, and money. As the city was rebuilt, people moved back. The new buildings were built to survive hurricane winds.

Today, Antony enjoys camping with his family near Alice Springs, Australia.

Antony's life now

Today, Antony works for the electric company that helped bring power back to Darwin after the cyclone. "I love Darwin," he says. "My boys are fascinated when they see photos of Darwin after Tracy hit."

New Orleans, Louisiana: 2005

On August 28, 2005, a storm in the Gulf of Mexico developed into a Category 5 hurricane. It headed toward the Louisiana and Mississippi coasts of the United States.

Chris's story

Eleven-year-old Chris Nungesser lived in a suburb of New Orleans, Louisiana. He was watching TV as a **meteorologist predicted** that Hurricane Katrina would hit New Orleans. "It freaked us out," Chris said. Everyone in the neighborhood began boarding up windows and gathering emergency supplies.

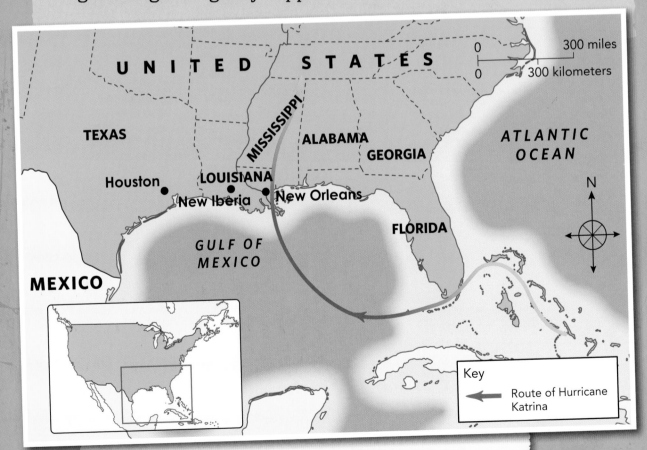

Hurricane Katrina hit Louisiana, Mississippi, and Alabama.

Leaving home

People were ordered to **evacuate**. About 960,000 out of 1.2 million people in New Orleans left the area. Chris and his family went to New Iberia, Louisiana. Roads were jammed with traffic.

When Chris reached New Iberia, he watched TV reports of rain gushing into the streets of New Orleans. **Dykes** surrounding the city had broken, and the streets filled with water.

Stuck in the city

Not everyone could leave New Orleans. Many who stayed were too old or sick to leave. Others were poor. They had no car, and public transportation was not working.

Floodwaters covered the city of New Orleans.

NUMBER CRUNCHING

In total, 1,833 people died because of Hurricane Katrina. In Louisiana, almost half of those who died were over 75 years old. Many were too sick or poor to leave their homes.

Temporary homes

Some **evacuees** stayed in **disaster centers** or were taken in by kind strangers. Others moved into temporary trailers provided by the Federal Emergency Management Agency (FEMA). Chris and his family moved in with an aunt and uncle in Houston, Texas. He began attending a school in Houston. The other children were kind, and the teachers were sympathetic.

The Astrodome sports stadium in Houston, Texas, was used as a disaster center to house hurricane evacuees.

Returning home

Chris flew home in mid-October. "Seeing the damage from above was frightening," he said. He saw boats and houses sprawled over roads. There was plenty of work ahead for the hurricane victims.

Chris's family was lucky. Even though the first floor of their house was damaged, it could be fixed. Sewer water had backed up in the pipes of their house. It stank.

People in Metairie, where Chris lived, used boats to travel through the flooded streets.

HELPING HAND

Talia Leman, of Iowa, was 10 years old when Hurricane Katrina struck New Orleans. She set up a website called RandomKid.org to raise money for hurricane victims. In the first three months, children raised more than $5 million for hurricane victims.

Total losses in New Orleans

Many people decided not to return to New Orleans. The city population dropped by 223,388 people within two years of the hurricane. About 205,000 houses were totally destroyed there.

Those who returned began repairing and rebuilding. However, many people who lived in poor neighborhoods lacked the money or supplies they needed to rebuild. They lived in FEMA trailers for years. By June 2010, nearly five years after the hurricane, there were still 350 FEMA trailers in New Orleans.

Many kids, such as 13-year-old Haylee Gaw of Kinnelon, New Jersey, helped to collect clothing and other supplies needed in New Orleans.

NUMBER CRUNCHING

More houses were lost in Hurricane Katrina than in any other natural disaster in U.S. history.

Beyond New Orleans

Because New Orleans is a major city, it received lots of coverage on television and in newspapers. However, Hurricane Katrina also damaged many other areas. The most damage occurred in Louisiana, Mississippi, and Alabama. Georgia, Florida, Kentucky, and Ohio also suffered damage from flooding.

Aisha Turner, age eight, lost her belongings in the hurricane. Here, she is searching through clothes at a relief center to find an outfit to wear to school.

HELPING HAND

Volunteers came from all over the United States to help with rebuilding. The Red Cross, Salvation Army, and Habitat for Humanity were among the many organizations to offer help. People from the rest of the world helped, too. Altogether, 70 nations offered aid.

Bangladesh: 2007

Cyclone Sidr, a powerful Category 4 hurricane, hit Bangladesh in November 2007. Over 3,000 people died. Most people died in floods caused by the **storm surge**.

Lamia's story

Seven-year-old Lamia and her family live near the coast of Bangladesh, in a village called Char Bangla. When her teacher warned that a cyclone was on the way, Lamia and five friends went door-to-door warning villagers to go to the cyclone shelter. Many did. But Lamia's father refused. Lamia grabbed his hand and pulled until he agreed to take shelter. Lamia and her friends saved many lives that day.

This map shows the route of Cyclone Sidr and the low-lying land that was flooded by the storm surge.

Ganges River

INDIA

BANGLADESH

INDIA

0   100 miles

0   100 kilometers

Key

← Route of Cyclone Sidr

Land flooded by storm surge

N

Bay of Bengal

MYANMAR

Dangerous play

Many homes and schools were damaged by the cyclone. Some children played among the **debris**. They searched for anything that might be useful. However, it was dangerous play. The debris included sharp items, pieces of metal, and even downed power lines.

Many houses in the villages of Bangladesh are not built out of strong materials. This woman's house was destroyed by the hurricane.

NUMBER CRUNCHING

It is thought that more than 80 percent of those killed by Cyclone Sidr were children. They were not able to swim or escape the storm surge fast enough. Many other children were injured or lost family members.

A terrible toll

During hurricanes, high winds and floods kill people and livestock, destroy buildings, and ruin crops. As a very poor country, Bangladesh is vulnerable to natural disasters. This is because families often have poor housing and not enough money to be able to leave an area if they are at risk.

Cyclone Sidr caused serious food and water shortages. In the weeks after the cyclone, people became ill by drinking unclean water. Others suffered from snakebites as they waded through floodwaters.

People waited for deliveries of clean water and food after the cyclone.

HELPING HAND

By June 2008, Save the Children had provided food to 176,000 families, medicine for 80,000 people, and provided safe play areas for 20,000 children in Bangladesh.

Bangladesh

Bangladesh experiences hurricanes, floods, and tornadoes. Almost all of Bangladesh lies only just above **sea level**. Most of its people are poor.

EUROPE

ASIA

Bangladesh

PACIFIC OCEAN

AFRICA

INDIAN OCEAN

Darwin

AUSTRALIA

Darwin, Australia

In 1974 Cyclone Tracy destroyed the city of Darwin, Australia.

ANTARCTICA

Glossary

air pressure weight of air pressing down on Earth. A change in air pressure indicates a change in the weather.

debris remains of things broken or destroyed; litter; garbage

disaster center protected area to sit out a natural disaster

dyke bank built to control or hold back the water of a sea or a river

engineer person who constructs or manages building projects

equator imaginary circle around Earth that is equally distant from the North Pole and South Pole

evacuate leave an area for reasons of safety

evacuee person who leaves an area for reasons of safety

evaporate give off moisture

jute strong, coarse fiber from a plant that grows in Asia

meteorologist person who studies the science behind the weather

moisture small amount of liquid that makes something wet

predict say that something will happen in the future, usually based on research or other information

radar way of detecting distant objects and determining their speed and position by turning radio waves into images

sea level level of the ocean's surface

seawall strong wall designed to prevent flooding from the sea

storm surge seawater pushed onto land by hurricane winds

tide rise and fall of the sea level on the shore

tropical cyclone massive storm that develops over warm ocean waters

wetlands land that has a wet and spongy soil, such as a marsh, swamp, or bog

Find Out More

Books

Chambers, Catherine. *Hurricane* (*Wild Weather*). Chicago: Heinemann Library, 2007.

Graf, Mike. *How Does a Cloud Become a Thunderstorm?* (*How Does It Happen?*). Chicago: Raintree, 2010.

Spilsbury, Louise, and Richard Spilsbury. *Howling Hurricanes* (*Awesome Forces of Nature*). Chicago: Heinemann Library, 2010.

Websites

http://eo.ucar.edu/webweather/hurricanehome.html
This is a fun website to learn about extreme weather, including games to play and activities to do.

www.fema.gov/kids/hurr.htm
This website tells what to do in the event of a hurricane.

www.randomkid.org
Set up by Talia Leman, this website provides support for those children who have been involved in a natural disaster. It also provides ways for children to help others who have suffered.

www.redcross.org/Katrina5Year
Visit this website to learn how the Red Cross has helped the victims of Hurricane Katrina.

http://skydiary.com/kids/hurricanes.html
Visit this website to find out information about hurricanes and how they are formed.

Index